MOUNTAIN MOVING DAY

poems by women
edited by Elaine Gill

The Crossing Press
Trumansburg, N.Y. 14886

Cover drawing and design by Dirck Bass
Photograph pages designed by Susan Porter

SBN 0-912278-36-6 (paper)
SBN 0-912278-37-4 (hardcover)
L.C. No. 73-77320

The Crossing Press Series
of Contemporary Anthologies

This project is supported by a grant from the National Endowment
for the Arts in Washington, D.C., a federal agency.

The mountain moving day is coming
I say so yet others doubt it
Only a while the mountain sleeps
In the past all mountains moved in fire
Yet you may not believe it
O man this alone believe
All sleeping women now awake and move
All sleeping women now awake and move.

Can you hear the river?
Canyons they stretch above it
But if you listen you can hear it below
Grinding stones into sand
Yet you may not hear it
O man this alone hear
All silent women scream in rage
All silent women scream in rage.

The mountain moving day is coming
I say so yet others doubt it
Only a while the mountain sleeps
In the past all mountains moved in fire
Yet you may not believe it
O man this alone believe
All sleeping women now awake and move
All sleeping women now awake and move
All sleeping women now awake and move.

1st verse: Yosano Akiko (1911)
2nd verse & song: © Naomi Weisstein, 1972,
for the Chicago Women's Liberation Rock Band.

CONTENTS

Introduction

Mountain Moving Day is a collection of poems written by 17 women, 5 from Canada and 12 from the U.S. It is contemporary. I didn't want to give an historical perspective on women poets— I wanted to present the picture now only. *Mountain Moving Day* is a small, fine collection of the best poems I could find.

I didn't have any axe to grind for or against Women's Liberation. Therefore the poems exhibit a variety of response to the current dilemna of women. Nor did I ask for poems exclusively to or for or about women.

In gathering the poems, I was astonished by their immense vitality and range. I do not believe women poets have a narrower range than men. Sure, the voice sometimes is sweet, but sometimes it is strident, the action an offensive against the oppressor, man. In other instances, the voice is sad or bitter, the discontent broadly directed. The range is there from rancor and invective to sweet paeans of happiness.

And the subjects of the poems are equally wide ranging. The women write about their lovers' bodies as men do. And they write about their children, if they have children, as men do. And they write about other people and places and abstract things just as men do.

I do not mean to say there is no difference between the poetry written by men and the poetry written by women. To me, there is an obvious difference, but that difference is no excuse for prejudice, for dismissing that different voice.

In the past women have tried to imitate the sound of men's voices. I remember in graduate school we tried hard not to be like women, that is, the image of women the men teachers had in their heads, but dryer—*safe* women. And as teachers, we had to assume the spinster mantle, like Athena, to keep the jobs. Thank God, it is going now.

Mountain Moving Day is truly upon us—women are beginning to speak out with their own voices. They are beginning to sound like women, making their own projections, their own pieces of living material, not out of their own bodies this time, but in words. And I think all of us, men and women, should be grateful for this new life that is upon us.

* * *

A word about the individual joys of this collection—
Alta's terse, pure lyrics; Margaret Atwood's celebration
of summer, the fullness of living, in "August"; Carol Berge's
cool jazz lyrics; Elizabeth Brewster's polite, controlled fury;
Carol Cox's interior landscapes; Susan Griffin's use of the
new form, the long poem, quite like the Russian long poems,
meant to be delivered orally, like conversation (Jessica Hagedorn
and Fran Winant also use this form with brilliance.);
Marie Harris's bitter sweet story of herbs, her kids, her
life; Erica Jong's incredible flow of image and word, a
real attempt to be popular and a good writer, like Colette;
Lyn Lifshin's great sad poem about a man and a woman, how
they meet and yet cannot meet; Pat Lowther's quiet history,
her observation post on middle class life; Marge Piercy's
vitality, her intellectual energy bursting out, recording her
life for us; Gwendolyn MacEwen, an original (like the painter
Rousseau) with her own vision, her own voice recording her
inner world with great accuracy and delicacy; Cathleen Quirk's
pure flute music stemming out of a wonderful coarseness;
Phyllis Webb's open-throated curses on cruel people, her
feeling for the poor victims; Kathleen Wiegner's "Proteus"
interpreting the modern psychic dilemma in classic terms.

* * *

I enjoyed choosing these poems and putting this volume
together. I hope you enjoy reading it.

Elaine Gill
Trumansburg, New York

ALTA

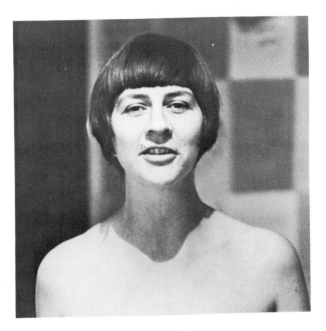

I operate Shameless Hussy Press where I print
and publish books I need. If you like my poems
herein, drop a note to me at Box 424, San
Lorenzo, California 94580. If you don't like
my poems, write to someone else.

Euridice

all the male poets write of orpheus
as if they look back & expect
to find me walking patiently
behind them. they claim i fell into hell.
damn them, i say.
i stand in my own pain
& sing my own song.

& Why Are All The Voices I Hear Divided Into Colors?

i come to you from a lonely place
far away & full of troubles.
& it's awful lonely out here i wish
you being man & me being woman
were no barrier i wish
our heads thot alike but
all those years of playboy
who can fight it   (can i)
with real skin & real breath & cries at nite
who can fight 2 lousy marriages   (can you)
& after all those bogeymen defeated,
our guts sliced open, do we yearn too hard /
4 days & nites alone too many all in a row
but now i'm lonely tho not alone & thats scary,
where is every body?   & whose hand
is that in mine?

Anybody Could Write This Poem. All You Have To Say Is Yes.

i'm happy.
could a pome be a cup
to pour our joy into?
you rubbing my hairy leg
& making me giggle
all our happy teeth
& tasting like love juice
& apples & bananas &
cheese & salami
we could do this over & over
& feel good over & over
the hot joy spilling
puddles on the bed, the rug,
the back yard, the earth
happy with us, needing our joy
& yes we say & we say yes
you whisper yesyesyes yes
yes. & yes.
& you feel good yes
& the hollow in yr shoulder
& i'm hungry for you yes
& yes. yes.
& why quit now when we could
say yes again why stop now
when we could yes why no when yes
love yes love yes love yes
earth. life. children. love.
yes. & yes to night & yes to
day to wake up & say yes.
the holy affirmation
to wake up wanting to be alive.

Pretty

—you know, Alta, yr roomate may be pretty, but
you have that inner beauty that counts— Barry, 1960

and here we are again, folks, a table of women, 7 of us, & the
first thing i do to assess my co-workers on Tooth & Nail is look
around at all of you to see who is prettier than i. my lover used to
say how i was prettier than other women in women's lib & i would
feel better while feeling worse & wish it weren't even a
consideration. in anybody's mind, including mine, because it
drives me crazy & actually prevents me from enjoying situations.
like i used to hate to go to martha's house because she is, and i
quote, perfectly beautiful. she doesn't even bite her nails. how
can i compete with that munch munch. then i got to know her &
the bitterness is real, cannot be measured; that we really like each
other & could have been friends all that awful lonely year but i
was afraid to be around her & have him look at my lousy skin &
big nose & bitten nails next to her perfect complexion & little
nose & nice nails. how could he possibly want me more than her?
everything becomes a handicap: every time i take a pill i think
jesus no man loves a sick wife (to quote mother). men don't
make passes at girls who wear glasses. blondes have more fun.
fat ass. big boobs. clear skin. sheeit.
   then it got so i could count on being the second prettiest
woman in any situation! sitting at the med i would always be able
to find one woman who was prettier & usually not more than one.
at any given party i could always see one woman who was prettier
& feel prettier than the rest. even on busses. even in classes.
doctors offices. restaurants. dances. no doubt it could have
carried over to skating rinks, art shows, family reunions, funerals.
we tried grading our looks one time. i gave myself 90 & the
therapist asked what would john rate you & i said lower & can you
imagine the bottom of that horrible fear? that each year i could only
become more afraid because now i've nursed 2 children; now my
throat is getting crepey (or whatever it's called); & my thighs will
never again be size 10 unless i get emaciated. a horrible fear
that drove me to a plastic surgeon who said all he could do with

my big nose was to hook it, drove me to try on 7 different bras
to nurse with so my boobs wouldnt hang low (do yr boobs hang
low? do they wobble to & fro?) drove me to dermatologists to
smooth out my skin, drove me to cover my face with makeup,
eyeliner, lipstick, mascara, drove me to curl & bleach my hair,
drove me to diet, drove me to sit with my fists clenched so no one
could see my nails. tell me i'm not oppressed. ask me what i
want. tell me you dont like my methods. listen to my life & see
that it has been intolerable & leave me the fuck alone.

Firebird ~ Alta

& i wanted to be inside you
& i wanted to fuck you
& crushed my titties into yr hair
my soft breast against you firm
in my hand & i wanted to fuck you,
to enter you, & pushing my breasts
into yr hair i tapped yr ass with
my finger, unwilling to hurt but
o so wanted you, wanting to fuck
you, my finger wanting to be in you,
my breasts hungry & i lap yr nipple &
you twist under me i push into you &
wing & press & come i come love &
we roll, you up now & humping open
so open you can ask & i can reach
to enter you again. & the flame wings
terrible soaring taste freedom flying
into flame & reborn our bodies wel-
coming (in the light of one small
candle yr beauty overwhelming).
come love and welcome
the resurrection of the body.

Stockton State Mental Hospital 1962

Shirley standing on the table
to see me thru the bars.
i cant hear thru double glass.
only see her mouth say
--they're sending me to juvenile hall, martinez.
her feet in white buck shoes & cotton socks.
she was so young
her breasts hurt when i touched them.

Shirley 4 Years Later

i was all self-righteous
when you came to visit
my overcleaned 3 bedroom home
in san lorenzo. yr baby
had diaper rash; i was superior;
my kid never even had a leaky nose.
your hair looked like mine does now.
you wore a white shirt, jeans, boots;
yr cigarette flapped on yr lip
as you talked. i sat primly shocked
& wondered why i ever (flash/ yr head in my lap
your delicate scarred fingertips on the back of
my neck, you pull me down & raise yr open mouth/
grass growing, trees, the brickbarred asylum, our kiss,
our kiss) why i ever hungered
for you, my legs crossed in my beige
carpeted living room.

The Art of Enforced Deprivation

i remember back in hi school
corliss & i were practicing dancing
i was the boy: my hand was around
her waist & the other holding her
hand. (that was how we danced back in those days)
her breast was poking me right there & i thot
"wow! boys sure get the good part!"

i looked at her face to see
if it felt as good to her as it did to me
but she wouldnt look at me.
i still dont know.

Don 1958

we were parked on a hill
warm in his blue chevvy
no houses over there.
he pulled me on his lap
his eyes closing with the
hot joy of it,
—o, sweets,
it never felt so good. . .

fighting my dependency:
keeping busy, having lunch
with friends, printing my book.
when you're away i feel like
i'm wearing one shoe.

i promised i would but i can't.
so what else is new?

how can people stand to be around me? i'm always babbling
about unity, life forces, the Deep Meaning of it All.
ugh i could live in constant embarrassment.

he asked me what was i fantasizing when i beat off in his friend's
                                        bathroom
& i knew what i was supposed to say so i said "i was thinking of
                                        you, dear"
but that was a lie.
i was just looking at my pretty titties
& feelin generally good.

a car has pulled up outside.
it is not for me, of course.
it has been a long time
since anyone loved me.

i slept alone last nite but when you know you dont have to,
its kind of an adventure. to just dream yr own dreams
& not wake up feeling
guilty

MARGARET ATWOOD

The difficulty is that I have no theories, poetic ones that is.
I suppose that you write from the center of where you happen
to be, and for me that includes (though I don't feel it's confined
by) being Canadian and female. Insofar as I think at all about my
work having a shape, it's the shape of an exploration (incomplete,
haphazard) of those still submerged territories. . . What do I "do"?
Too much involvement with outside things . . . help run a small
experimental press, other kinds of writing, teach when I have to.

Fishbowl

You are curious, you wish
to step through the mirror
into this place where I live reversed,
someone's twin or moon

It may be a window, it may be an aquarium,
it may be thin ice,
whether I breathe light or water
you can't tell from there.

What do you want? A mermaid
with squid hair,
a cigar-box lady, velvet fat and gilt paper?
It's your soul, decide please,
I don't do this for fun.

I float silently, barbed as a lure,
attentive as your reflection;
mineral flower grown
in a bowl, stone almost human.

Risk it, put your hand through
this cold illusion, this glass:
I will break or not break, you will drown
or not drown, either way
you will know what I am.

There is Only One Of Everything

Not a tree but the tree
we saw, it will never exist, split by the wind and bending down
like that again. What will push out of the earth

later, making it summer, will not be
grass, leaves, repetition, there will
have to be other words. When my

eyes close language vanishes. The cat
with the divided face, half black half orange
nests in my scruffy fur coat, I drink tea,

fingers curved around the cup, impossible
to duplicate these flavours. The table
and freak plates glow softly, consuming themselves,

I look out at you and you occur
in this winter kitchen, random as trees or sentences,
entering me, fading like them, in time you will disappear

but the way you dance by yourself
on the tile floor to a trite song, flat and mournful,
so delighted, spoon waved in one hand, wisps of roughened hair

sticking up from your head, it's your surprised
body, pleasure I like. I can even say it,
though only once and it won't

last: I want this. I want
this.

First Prayer

In these prayers let us not forget our bodies
which were loyal most of the time
though they would have preferred freedom;

They stood in rows when we lined them up,
they ate when we told them to, when the food was bad
they didn't complain, they wore our livery,
our utensils, grey animal fur hands
on their hands, blades on their feet,
they let us warp them
for purposes of display or science

and so many of them are roaming around empty
in parks and standing idle on corners
because their owners have abandoned them
in favour of word games or jigsaw puzzles.

In spite of it all they forgive us
again and again, they heal their own wounds
and ours too, they walk upright for us
when we ourselves are crippled,
they touch each other, perform love in our place
and for our sake, we who are numbed and disabled;

and they are discreet, they keep our secret,
with their good help we will rise from the dead.

 O body, descend
 from the wall where I have nailed you
 like a flayed skin or a war trophy

 Let me inhabit you, have compassion on me
 once more, give me this day.

First Element

i)

Eating fire

is your ambition:
to swallow the flame down
take it into your mouth
and shoot it forth, a shout or an incandescent
tongue, a word
exploding from you in gold, crimson,
unrolling in a brilliant scroll

To be lit up from within
vein by vein

To be the sun

(Taught by a sideshow man)

ii)

Dead man by the roadside
thrown from the overturning
truck or hit by something, a car, a bullet

On his head the hair glows,
the blood inside ignited,
short blue thorns of flame still flickering over him

Was it worth it? ask him.
(Did you save anyone?)

He gets up and walks away, the fire
growing on him like fur

iii)

Here the children have a custom. After the celebration of evil they
take those vacant heads that shone once with such anguish
and glee and throw them over the bridge, watching the smash, orange,
as they hit below. We were standing underneath when you told it.

People do that with themselves when they are finished, light scooped
out. He landed here, you said, marking it with your foot.

You wouldn't do it that way, empty, you wouldn't wait, you would
jump with the light still in you.

iv)

This is your trick or miracle,
to be consumed and rise
intact, over and over, even for myths there is
a limit, the time when you accomplish
failure and return
from the fire minus your skin.

The new eyes are golden and
maniac, a bird's or lion's

Through them you see
everything, as you wished,
each object (lake, tree, woman)

transfigured with your love, shining
in its life, its pain, like waves, tears, ice,
like flesh laid open to the bone.

v)

To be the sun, moving through space

distant and indifferent, giving
light of a kind for those watching

To learn how to
live this way. or not. to choose

to be also human, the body
mortal and faded, incapable of saving

itself, praying
as it falls. in its own way.

You Are Happy

The water turns
a long way down over the raw stone,
ice crusts around it

We walk separately
along the hill to the open
beach, unused
picnic tables, wind
shoving the brown waves, erosion, gravel
rasping on gravel.

In the ditch a deer
carcass, no head. Bird
running across the glaring
road against the low pink sun.

When you are this
cold you can think about
nothing but the cold, the images

hitting into your eyes
like needles, crystals, you are happy.

Late August

This is the plum season, the nights
blue and distended, the moon
hazed, this is the season of peaches

with their lush lobed bulbs
that glow in the dusk, apples
that drop and rot
sweetly, their brown skins veined as glands

No more the shrill voices
that cried   Need   Need
from the cold pond, bladed
and urgent as new grass

Now it is the crickets
that say   Ripe   Ripe
slurred in the darkness while the plums

dripping on the lawn outside
our window, burst
with a sound like thick syrup
muffled and slow

The air is still
warm, flesh moves over
flesh, there is no

hurry

CAROL BERGE

I think all of us are conditioned quite early on about sex roles, esp. what we can and cannot do, and most women are taught not to try to achieve as minds, but to watch and wait while the men go and do. Well—in

the words of the immortal Lady Murasaki, fuck that; I like to be busy and "the mind is a muscle," people are interesting, my business as it has most naturally turned out is in describing this era, and I'm glad I'm good at it. I also like men very much and wish they were more aware of their ability to be affectionate and gentle, contrary to their conditioning; they seem to be too busy hustling the warrior bit along to enjoy each other, us, and themselves. . . This is an era inhabited by fear but also by Change. Some people are afraid of joy but that too changes.

(To His Coy Mistress)
:
Lying Down Hungry

come darling
be my scapegoat
let me tell you
all the things
that have been wrong
with my whole life
and blame you
and thus
get rid of them
forever

of course i realize
i may also get rid of you
this way
but it is a
calculated risk
because you are
so vulnerable and
so willing and
so handy

These things have
been with me too long
longer than you
and you see
i can only rid myself
by putting my mouth
or body
to yours

i will miss you
all
but i have no choice
stand still i said
darling

Madonna & Daughter

(for Bunuel)

the strangled child, forty years old, old,
walks modern sunday mexico with her mama.
another sunday: they are together: lunch,
window-shopping, not as friends. together.
the taller daughter wears costly pink silk.
her no-seam stockings define ankleless legs
which match her mother's walk precisely.
the same profile, chins of flesh, stance,
mouths sameset. the firm mother is sixty,
strong, sad, arrogant. herself strangled,
the invisible leashes held taut. the way
they differ: she has this child, her image,
and holds a tether: a choked new virgin.
too late for chins to scream 'too late!'
too gone, into a resemblance. just years
ahead, as equal as sunday from spain to now.
forty more years, twenty of them all sunday,
valor bred out, meaningless legs and chins
corseted into a life, peering the chasm down.

Textures

the hunchbacked woman:
clad in bright silk.
her hair shining near
her lover's cheek.

if the flawed flower has
fine perfume and true
color, it rouses the
senses. she knows this.

what is between them,
their legs, has contentment.
perhaps the color of
that silk, her silken hair.

Where It's At

(for Adrianne Gornick)

told me and told me
for five weeks
about her new man
she told me he
is this he is
that and the
sixth week she
lays it on me he
is a spade cat
a negro you dig yes
well last week
tells me they turned on
and this cat of hers
who is negro and
getting a doctorate
at hah-vahd
well like when
he was high he
went into a low
nigra drawl he
sing out he say to her
i nuthin but some
kinda nigger whut you
want wid me
you ofay chick and
he break into a
little buck & wing
right there
there in the street
under the streetlight
amid the metal roses
of the bowerie

Blues For A Cello Man

He never talk enough
but when he come
he scream
and grab my thigh so tight
it make a big blue bruise

I like my men
                talky and
                        tender

Rested Near Nefertete:

                            nothing could
prevent her from being photographed,
in her bird-feather-caped isolation.
Smooth priest-cheeks slept near
her hammock, in it. We think
animals walked wild over her place;
it cannot be proven.
                        It is said
she is seen at the Gare St. Lazare
information desk, in a finality
of white robes. Her peacepipe
advertises papal bulls, framed in
mother-of-pearl: for pink walls of
the private trains of the princesses.

Poem For Explorers

At the Museum of Natural History
in New York, I see my Aunt Ethel.
She is standing, near you, in the
midst of the Amazon Rain Forest.
You are both behind glass; backed
by the bird-calls of that region.
Quite life-like; really uncanny.
You are both chewing on human bones.
She holds her husband's thighbone.
You have mine. From here, I notice
you yourself seem to be limping.
What injury? Who, then, has yours?
is marching, even as you, somewhere?
And do they have rallies for peace,
on the intrafamilial level, in the
forest of the Amazon rain-belt? Or
is the balance of nature sufficient?

With

it was a yearlong bloodbath it was
a time of incessant hammering with
no humor it was heat as melting as
death made palpable my bleachbones
merging in the furnace of with you
it was clear singsong of lunacy as
contagious as leprous islanders as
caught and netted as the foolishly
iridescent fish near island reef my
eyes impaled on a knife of with you
yes it was no no a yearlong trip as
red time of convulsive melting with
no charity save heat as burning for
death made tasty prepared like some
smart pie of leprous eyes whitened
like small bones in the furnaces of
with you on island of you with fire

Third Day In A Strange City

may i slobber over you
i havent spoken to anyone for three days
and am irrevocably lonely
from lack of communication

could i do you think
sit at table which is your eyes
a brief time
just long enough to regain my perspective

just long enough for some sustenance
you see i left my doctor at home
my child is in another country
my parents just left on a ship

my brother is married to someone else
and so is my oncebeloved husband
my friends all talk to each other
but they are in another city

there are too many hills here dont you think
tell me something about your young times
your cabins or shells or music
anything you choose

Position — *Carol Berge*

i stand before you
to represent all of the women
you have ever hated

your mother who
whipped the shit out of you
your aunt who
kibitzed the life out of your life
the girl who didnt
or wouldnt or couldnt   but didnt
etc   etc   etc

what chance have i got
unless you consider
that you stand before me too

ELIZABETH BREWSTER

I'm not sure what to say, and am inclined to let the poems
speak for themselves. I've published five books of poems,
the most recent being PASSAGE OF SUMMER (1969) and
SUNRISE NORTH (1972). I'm working on another collection
of poems and on a novel. I held a Canada Council Arts Award
in 1971-2; am at present teaching here at the University of
Saskatchewan.

Disqualification

I am of puritan and loyalist ancestry
and of middle class tastes.
My father never swore in front of ladies,
as he always quaintly called women.
My mother thought that a man was no gentleman
if he smoked a cigar without asking her permission;
and she thought all men should be gentlemen,
even though a gentleman would not call himself one,
and all women should be ladies,
even though a lady would not call herself one.

I have never taken any drug
stronger than aspirin.
I have never been more than slightly drunk.
I think there are worse vices
than hypocrisy or gentility,
or even than voting Conservative.

If I wanted to be fucked
I should probably choose a different word.
(Anyhow, I am not quite sure
whether it is a transitive or an intransitive verb,
because it was never given to me to parse.)

Usually I can parse words, analyze sentences,
spell, punctuate,
and recognize the more common metrical forms.

It is almost impossible
that I shall ever be
a truly established poet.

The Princess Addresses The Frog Prince

Oh, Frog Prince, Frog Prince,
it was not for you
that I dropped my golden ball
down into the deep water.

It was only by chance
that I dropped it at all.
I intended to stand still
holding the ball safe in my hand
and to look at myself reflected
with my gold crown on my hair
in the pond's surface.

Never in all the stories
was there a more beautiful princess.

And when the ball slipped
and fell from my hand
among the water lilies,
if I expected anyone to rise
from beneath the water

it was a merman or a drowned prince
who would be brought to life
by my eyes.

Never mind, you have a fine voice.
I will take you out of the water
to play in my garden.
I will even take you into the palace.
You shall sit by my gold plate
at dinner time
and be my ugly pet
and sing me songs.

On Reading Another Poet

I think we are being given the same messages
that oracles are speaking in our dreams
warning admonition code
syllables of unknown meaning.

We are not in competition.
If I say the same thing
it is not because I copy
but because the voice says so.

Maybe there will be hundreds of us
like choric echoes.
It will not matter
that the words repeat themselves

so long as what is said
rises like the tide in all our separate waves
and beats upon and shapes the dreaming shore.

Moon

Was it not the goddess of the moon
who destroyed Actaeon in her forests?
He came too close to her, he gazed
without protection at her nakedness.

She turned him into a wild stag,
and his own hounds
his servants
leaped at his throat and killed him.

Was it not his fault,
the foolish man
who came into the moon's forests,
who climbed the moon's mountain,
who looked too close
at the naked moon?

For The Unknown Goddess

Lady, the unknown goddess,
we have prayed long enough only
to Yahweh the thunder god.

Now we should pray to you again
goddess of a thousand names and faces
Ceres Venus Demeter Isis
Inanna Queen of Heaven
or by whatever name
you would be known

you who sprang from the sea
who are present in the moisture of love
who live in the humming cells
of all life
who are rain
with its million soft fingers

and you who are earth
you with your beautiful ruined face
wrinkled by all
that your children have done to you.

sunlike lady
crowned with the whirling planets.

Lady of peace, of good counsel,
of love, of wisdom

we invoke your name
which we no longer know

and pray to you
to restore our humanity
as we restore your divinity.

CAROL COX

I left Wyoming a few months ago, where I had lived just west of the Bighorn Mountains and taught in an institution for delinquent boys. Before that I lived in New York City. I have come back home now, to the South. The man I share my life with and I are living in the country outside of Jackson, Mississippi, in the

mostly Black community of Tougaloo. Being back here, "back" meaning both down the dirt road which leads to our house and in the part of the country where I spent most of my life, feels right and good to me, as though I will be free of superfluous "needs," to try to come to know intimately just what my obligations are, to the people I love and the place where I live, and to myself. I think the South is a workable place to live, a continual birthing, and I think I should not try to displace the roots of the emotional attachment I feel to it. I want most, I guess, to be useful to the people who move around me and in whom I am contained, and to feel peaceful, not chafed, about the place where I live, so that I may be useful to it, too; and it is in that context that I view my writing.

From The Direction Of The State Mental Institution

comes a crackling noise, a kind of chirping
which you can't hear any better
if you put your ear to the ground,

and then you might be rolled
into a category and stamped
with a capital letter. but meanwhile

the noise prevents sleep, follows
just far enough away
to stick like sap. you will

do anything except go nearer,
you will recite poems you don't
even know loudly and offer

proposals of marriage to faces
which keep trying to place you.
that is the end

of the story of your life
out on the sidewalk on an empty spot
near which ants have planted

tiny points of old food.

Papa Doc Is Dead

A man walks quietly through the bank
murmuring that the enemy is near.
Those who hear slip away
to a storage bin filled with molasses and rice

where they dream long, cool dreams
of velvet women.
When the earth above them
pounds and sways,

they wake, terrified that
the women's bites have left them rabid.

In fifty years
they will lurch out
into the cold sunlight
and find the island shrunk
to the size of a napkin

full of voices
knocking about on the wind.

Watching You Draw

Bent over those
dark threads of ink,
your back is thin and fair

as a cattail
leaning under the weight
of a red-winged blackbird.

The old lamp I read under
sends you smoking colors
you do not need but use,
folding them into
your shadowed corner.

Your back is a network
of hollow birds,
false gold,
and marginal lines held tight across
the throats of pretenders.

All Three Of Us

Driving home from the School
you are bitter and sad
because you have hurt a child
knowing that you had to
to help make him whole

knowing you love him
with a fierce angry devotion
and must hold the burden
        of his ignorance in your brain

                    * * *

This evening standing near the frozen marsh
touching the last bit of sun
that leans toward us
the wind over our knees

Your hands are heavier
moving across me
than ever before, fearful
of losing of disappearing

fearful that my skin
will betray you

and waiting for the child's face
for the air to condense
but even if it does
all three of us can get through

can get through because
the parts of us are interchangeable
and confusing to the elements

How The Indians Lost The Hot Springs

No one told them about the disease,
how it crawled over the mountains
leaving wood too poisoned
to use for fire;

how survivors were insane
and armed with heavy stones;

how the green and red-brown water plants
were the only cure.

Men in high bright buildings
painted their faces gold
in exchange for the waters.
Their skin gleamed in the sun.
At night, one whispered to another
that he felt he was smothering to death.

He Left The Pine Ridge Reservation

because the land was shifting, dying,
over his feet:
unbroken earth for all that time
and then no going back.

Went west, to try to chase
the sorrow down. His thick hair
grew waist-long in a day.
Visions came:
turquoise wings with iron tips
circling the buttes, dim and quiet.
He wrote them down;
the paper turned to ash.

Just before the Utah line,
he stole some gas
for the rusting car; the man
ran him down.
Inside the jail
he pressed his arms
against the walls
to hold back the length of grief
that was bearing down.

Once he would have sung
his dreams to himself,
those secrets worth keeping.
Now he only thought
of how he loathed this state,
this town, and
where it would deliver him.

SUSAN GRIFFIN

A daughter, granddaughter, mother with generations of
words and weeping and howling and giggling and screaming
and laughter kept silent now emerging in poetry and
stories. Wrote a book of poems called DEAR SKY, and
one called THREE POEMS FOR WOMEN. Escapes
starvation, full employment, wifehood, suicide, boredom,
imprisonment, (capture), doesn't know much more, riding
with each wave, barely.

Grenadine

The movies, she told me
ruined my life.
we were sitting there
drinking bourbon and soda
flavored by grenadine.
I in the leather chair
that engulfed me
carrying me back,
on the television
a late movie
we weren't watching,
its noise took up our silences.
she was fat from all her drinking
and her eyes darted
unfocused about the room
her voice jumped from deep
to high laughter.
Really, she said,
no kidding, she said,
I mean that,
the movies, she said
curling her lip
and looking meanly
at George Sanders
on the T.V.
"They," she said
pointing and accusing
"tell you things about life
that aren't true."
she sat staring a long time
trying to focus on my eyes.
"Hello, sweetie,"she said
and smiled at me
like a cockeyed hula dancer
from inside a ukelele.
She put her glass
embellished with splashes of
gold on the metal T.V. tray
her feet on the leather stool.

She had it fixed
so she never had to move.

"Your father," she said
"he was a good man,
do you know why
we di-
vorced?"
"No,"
I stared at the
grenadine in my bourbon.
"Because of the movies,"
she said.
I blinked past her eyes
heaved in the leather chair
trying to upright myself
trying to refill my glass,
the television
busily selling cars,
my step-father snoring on
the couch
like a giant vacuum cleaner.
she laughed
a high-pitched laugh and tried
her very best
to stare right at me.
"We would go to the movies
your father and I."
I nodded at her.
"And I'd come out
being Carol Lombard,
only he refused
to be Humphrey Bogart."
We stared at each other
the television
sticking to the sides of our faces
George Sanders pretending to be
evil pretending to be good
being unmasked by
Rosalind Russell pretending

to be a lady reporter
pretending in real life
all she really wanted was
a home and family she said
to Ladies Home Journal reporter but
job of acting and stardom
thrust upon her
never found right man.

"All the myths," my mother
said. "I saw a movie"
about, about
they made me think, she said
running off with another man
would be African jungle
beautiful in dark green
Don Ameche canoeing to
palace in wilderness
speaking mad poetry
of love
absolute lusty
freedom of it all
glorious spirit of man
kissing
in white bow tie
and unconquerable
white orchid
marachino cherry red lips
she said
they made it look so glamorous
drinking her grenadine bourbon
and fell asleep,
my step-father snoring
on the couch,
while the dog
whined outside the screen door
to be let in.

An Answer To A Man's Question, "What Can I Do About Women's Liberation?"

Wear a dress.
Wear a dress that you made yourself, or bought in a dress
store.
Wear a dress and underneath the dress wear elastic, around
your hips, and underneath your nipples.
Wear a dress and underneath the dress wear a sanitary napkin.
Wear a dress and wear sling back, high heeled shoes.
Wear a dress, with elastic and a sanitary napkin underneath,
and sling back shoes on your feet, and walk down telegraph
avenue .
Wear a dress, with elastic and a sanitary napkin and sling
back shoes on telegraph avenue and try to run.

Find a man.
Find a nice man who you would like to ask you for a date.
Find a nice man who will ask you for a date.
Keep your dress on.
Ask the nice man who asks you for a date to come to dinner.
Cook the nice man a nice dinner so the dinner is ready before
he comes and your dress is nice and clean and wear a smile.
Tell the nice man you're a virgin, or you don't have
birth control, or you would like to get to know him better.
Keep your dress on.
Go to the movies by yourself.

Find a job.
Iron your dress.
Wear your ironed dress and promise the boss you won't get
pregnant (which in your case is predictable) and you like to
type, and be sincere and wear your smile.
Find a job or get on welfare.
Borrow a child and get on welfare.
Borrow a child and stay in the house all day with the child,
or go to the public park with the child, and take the child
to the welfare office and cry and say your man left you and
be humble and wear your dress and your smile, and don't talk
back, keep your dress on, cook more nice dinners, stay
away from telegraph avenue, and still, you won't know the
half of it, not in a million years.

JESSICA TARAHATA HAGEDORN

I was born in the Philippines 24 years ago, a
writer-actress-musician; co-editor of THIRD WORLD
WOMEN: AN ANTHOLOGY (Third World Commu-
nications Press). My poetry will appear this year in
FOUR YOUNG WOMEN: AN ANTHOLOGY
(Herder & Herder Press) to be edited by Kenneth
Rexroth. My play CHIQUITA BANANA has been
produced by NET and I am now working on a new
collection of poems tentatively titled LIVE MUSIC.
As for the revolution—it is like music—always in the
air I breathe. . .

Autobiography Part Two: Rock and Roll

Dedicated to the poet Victor Hernandez Cruz

We boogied when I was eight
I had just learned to dance
Carl Perkins sang 'Matchbox'
And I hated him

But anything was better
Than Bill Haley or Frankie Laine
Until Elvis and Little Richard;

I wanted them so much
I would've known how to fuck them then
In joyous appreciation

When I was ten
It was Etta James
I didn't know what she looked like,
If she were male or female

I worried about my odor
When I did the slowdrag
And the guys had their
Sideways erections
To Etta James

And then
Chubby Checkers and Joey Dee
Red shirts stained with sweat

Tight white toreador pants

American tennis shoes—

In 1960 Elvis was a drag
Harry Belafonte gave a concert
At the Coliseum
The older chicks dug him.
(He wore a beautiful tangerine
Shirt open at the throat)

Fabian was doing his tiger
We posed for a photograph
Together
Cost me three pesos
And an autographed lace
Handkerchief

1962 and Philadelphia Italians
Fabian Frankie Avalon Dion and the Belmonts
With poufed blond hair

I was in Hongkong
Buying Bobby Vee records
And then Tokyo
Buying Paul Anka
"Live at the Copacabana"

San Francisco
was a gray dream
A gray meat market harbor

I thought it was Chicago

My mother cried
A lot then

Her face was gray

The Four Seasons were very big
For some reason
I hated them

They weren't even
A good shuck.

My first weeks in
San Francisco and I was
Surrounded by faggots;
Lovely gilt-frame
Antique faggots:

My uncles   my mothers
My dubious friends—

Bill Haley was dead
Bobby Vee was dead
Little Richard in some church

Yes, yes Little Anthony
Was very big then . . .

I will never forget him.

Smokey's Gettin' Old

for Smokey Robinson

hey Nellie,
            you wearin' your hair up too high
hair spray   showin clotted white   against your blackness

            (lyin' in the sun   i wait for the crow to scream)

hey Nellie,
            how long you been here?   did you come with your daddy
in 1959   on a second-class boat   cryin' all the while

cause you didn't want to leave the barrio
the girls back there
                who wore their hair loose   lots of orange
lipstick and movies on Sundays,   Quiapo market in the morning,
your grandma chewin' red tobacco—roast pig   (yeah, and it
tastes good. . .)
                hey Nellie,   did ya have to live in Stockton
with your daddy, and talk to old farmers who immigrated in 1941;
did your daddy promise you to a fifty-eight year old bachelor
who stank of cigars and   did you
                            run away to San Francisco

    go to Poly High, rat your hair hang around Woolworth's
Chinatown at 3 in the morning
          go to the Cow Palace and catch
     Smokey Robinson
         cry at his gold jacket dance
every Friday night at the Mission go steady with Ruben (your
daddy can't stand it cause he's a Spik)
         and the sailors
you dreamed of in Manila with yellow hair did they
     take you to the beach to ride the ferris wheel

     Life's Never Been So Fine!
You
  and Carmen harmonize "Be My Baby" by the Ronettes
and 1965 you get laid at a party Carmen's house
and Ruben marries you and you give up harmonizin'
   (lyin' in the sun i wait for the crow to scream;
at the university long-haired professors jack-off to Stendhal
and Proust)
      Nellie, you sleep without dreams
and remember the barrios and how it's all the same
Manila the Mission Chinatown L.A. Fillmore street
and you're gettin' kinda fat and Smokey Robinson's gettin' old
but your son has learned to jive to the Jackson 5
(lyin' in the sun i think about San Francisco and i wish i could
take the crow home with me)
        i don't want to
        but i love you
        it seems that i'm always
        thinkin' of you
        though you do me wrong babe
        my love is strong babe
        you really got a hold on me

Kayumangi

What it is
       gold eyelids
               dancing

& my man gone

What it is
      "taste"
           quietness

lady
   that's what they say
        I shd be

but
   What it is

              my music
              my color
              my face
              the loudness
                      of my bracelets
              clanging

Is/
   my soul
   my man
      here

MARIE HARRIS

It is as though the secret is in the repetition, as
though by doing things over and over I find out how
to do them. I am my mother's daughter. I am the
mother of my sons. I am a writer. I am a teacher.
My reality looks something like yours, looks a lot
like mine last year or next year over and over.
Beginning again, one more time, the repetition of
my life, I might make one new thing and repeat it.
Breaking and entering just to have a look around
. . . maybe changing the position of one object in
the room or dumping a kitchen drawer . . . to
have been there and left and come back.

Song

Hair
like heather, father would boast,
when my feet were still
soft and my breath
sweet as a calf's.

When the eyes of cows
reproached me, when
the girls swelled for love
of their boys, I left,

learned other skills
and carried the coals
of my efficiency all over
the city. I pleased
more than one man
that way.

Father, my fingers are cold.
I have no heart
or song in this town.
My men go home at night
and I am not pretty

not pretty any more.

Monkshood

> —took his name of the Greeke word signifying corruption,
> poison, or death—

she pulled me out the kitchen door
to see them
the deadly spring flowers
wonderful
purple

I have been waiting for you all afternoon

Facts Of Winter

The thermometer is not to be believed;
facts in winter are noisier than that.
The trees yip like dogs and the wind screeches
one skid after another.
Have you listened
to the frozen apples banging?
Don't shout! The cloud avalanche is massing.
Will you ever forget the winter of '71 . . .
sure, we all have our stories—bursting pipes,
strangers huddled in the Texaco station, electrical
cutbacks, states of emergency, what have you—
but did I tell you how
my friends and I became separated
between here and the barn?

Learning

At Spearfish, S.D. once
the temperature took a freakish jump
from -4 F. to 45 F.
in two minutes.
I wanted

to be in those minutes,
feeding chickens maybe
or sanding the walk,
when they hit;

inside, where fish survive
on promises
and the skin
feels itself.

Visitors

If you had not heard of the northward migration
of the Brazilian killer bee, loosed inadvertently
by a greedy honey baron, you would have slept that
much easier. It's the way with all pieces of surprising
information. Your life is changed daily and as
arbitrarily as a traffic light, and your marriage lies
dormant for as long as an alligator pear pit on
toothpicks. Leave the food on your plate. Someone will
eat it.

Luxury Apt

It never gets dark. Crickets suffocate with little
clicks in the air conditioning. Where are the creaking
boards, the window pane that rattles? Light without
sun. Airplanes or busses opening into terminals. There
has been a strike or a storm, some foul-up no one understands,
though rumors fly, and we grow roots in our places in line.
We are plane trees chewing concrete, swaying in smoke,
                              blossoming under
fluorescence, watching the cat. And when the cat rolls over
stiff legged and wheezing, we know we have less than an hour
to get out.

Dill

(for William and Sebastian)

The young cat knew enough to lick her firstborn, but
she didn't know enough to stop.

I trusted nothing
but the boring fists and elbows
my muscles made: that fact
and the facts of William and Sebastian Matthews.
My instincts ran to violence, ocelots
on leather leashes,
untrustworthy.

It was learning another way to walk, one hand
in front of the other.

My neighbors grow acres of Romilar,
Enfamil, Kaopectate, A&D Ointment,
Pampers, paregoric,
St. Joseph's

and I grow dill because it stalks the garden
taller than anything
and the split seeds stain my fingernails.
Dill water. For hiccoughs.
For sleep.
You two will drink anything
believing it's my strange lullaby
and I love you.

Lemon Balm

—Pliny saith that it is of so great vertue, that though
it be but tied to his sword that hath given the wound,
it stauncheth the blood.—John Gerard

It is well to plant balm about places where bees are
kept; they find their way home by it.

I never
want to see you again.

And this Peruvian remedy for indigestion:
Toast a slice of bread until it is charred black.
Put the charred bread and some fresh balm leaves into a cup;
add boiling water
and steep for about five minutes.
Pour the liquid off.
That should keep you busy.

The nightmare of having a family.
The nightmare of not having a family.

This harsh lemony herb
is probably as effective as anything
against the biting of mad dogs.

If I were a witch and you came to me late at night and furtive,
I might give you wine with lemon balm against the night and
terror and the throbbing of your gums; I might turn you away.

When I had bees swarming in my hair you were afraid
to touch me. Now though, I only have bees in my hair.

ERICA JONG

Perhaps my "Dear Colette" poem comes closest to say-
ing what I feel about writing at this point in my life.
I used to admire those writers who died young & went
down in a blaze of self-destructive glory (Plath,
Chatterton, even Byron & Dylan Thomas). Now I am
much more devoted to those who endured, like Colette.
It is easier, in a way, to kiss the world a bitter goodbye
than to go on working, writing, changing, enduring the
slings & arrows of outrageous aging. Colette endured.
And she wrote & wrote & wrote. Whenever I feel really
depressed, I think of her & keep going.

Dearest Man-In-The-Moon

ever since our lunch of cheese
& moonjuice
on the far side of the sun,
I have walked the craters of New York,
a trail of slime
ribboning between my legs,
a phosphorescent banner
which is tied to you,
a beam of moonlight
focussed on your navel,
a silver chain
from which my body dangles,
& my whole torso chiming
like sleighbells in a Russian novel.

Dearest man-in-the-moon,
I used to fear moonlight
thinking her my mother.
I used to dread nights
when the moon was full.
I used to scream
"Pull down the shade!"
because the moonface leered at me,
because I felt her mocking,
because my fear lived in me
like rats in a wheel of cheese.

You have eaten out my fear.
You have licked
the creamy inside of my moon.
You have kissed
the final crescent of my heart
& made it full.

Colder

He was six feet four, and forty-six, and
even colder than he thought he was.
      —James Thurber,The Thirteen Clocks

Not that I cared about the other women.
Those perfumed breasts with hearts
of pure rock salt.
Lot's wives—
all of them.

I didn't care
if they fondled him at parties,
eased him in at home
between a husband & a child,
sucked him dry
with vacuum cleaner kisses.

It was the coldness that I minded,
though he'd warned me.
"I'm cold," he said—
(as if that helped any).
But he was colder
than he thought he was.

Cold sex.
A woman has to die
& be exhumed
four times a week
to know the meaning of it.
His lips are razors,
his pelvic bones are knives,
even his elbows could cut butter.

Cold flows from his mouth
like a cloud of carbon dioxide.
His penis is pure dry ice

which turns to smoke.
His face hangs over my face—
an ice carving.

One of these days
he'll shatter
or
he'll melt.

Sunjuice

What happens when the juice of the sun
drenches you
with its lemony tang, its tart sweetness
& your whole body stings with singing
so that your toes sing to your mouth
& your navel whistles to your breasts
& your breasts wave to everyone
as you walk down the summer street?

What will you do
when nothing will do
but to throw your arms around trees
& men
& to greet every woman as sister
& to run naked in the spray of the fire hydrants
with children of assorted colors?

Will you cover your drenched skin
with woolen clothes?
Will you wear a diaper of herringbone tweed?
Will you piece together a shroud of figleaves
& lecture at the University
on the Lives of the Major Poets,
the History of Despair in Art?

Dear Colette

Dear Colette,
I want to write to you
about being a woman
for that is what
you write to me.

I want to tell you how your face
enduring after thirty, forty, fifty . . .
hangs above my desk
like my own muse.

I want to tell you how your hands
reach out from your books
& seize my heart.

I want to tell you how your hair
electrifies my thoughts
like my own halo.

I want to tell you how your eyes
penetrate my fear
& make it melt.

I want to tell you
simply that I love you—
though you are "dead"
& I am still "alive."

                    *

Suicides & spinsters—
all our kind!
Even decorous Jane Austen
never marrying,
& Sappho leaping,
& Sylvia in the oven,
& Anna Wickham, Tsvetaeva, Sara Teasdale,
& pale Virginia floating like Ophelia
& Emily alone, alone, alone. . . .

But you endure & marry,
go on writing,
lose a husband, gain a husband,
go on writing,
sing & tap dance
& you go on writing,
have a child & still
you go on writing,
love a woman, love a man
& go on writing.
You endure your writing
& your life.

                *

Dear Colette,
I only want to thank you:

for your eyes ringed
with bluest paint like bruises,
for your hair gathering sparks
like brush-fire,
for your hands which never willingly
let go,
for your years, your child, your lovers,
all your books . . . .

Dear Colette,
you hold me
to this life.

Becoming A Nun

On cold days
it is easy to be reasonable,
to button the mouth against kisses,
dust the breasts
with talcum powder
& forget
the red pulp meat
of the heart.

On those days
it beats
like a digital clock—
not a beat at all
but a steady whirring
chilly as green neon,
luminous as numerals in the dark,
cool as electricity.

& I think:
I can live without it all—
love with its blood pump,
sex with its messy hungers,
men with their peacock strutting,
their silly sexual baggage,
their wet tongues in my ear
& their words like little sugar suckers
with sour centers.

On such days
I am zipped in my body suit,
I am wearing seven league red suede boots,
I am marching over the cobblestones
as if they were the heads of men,

& I am happy
as a seven-year-old virgin
holding Daddy's hand.

Don't touch.
Don't try to tempt me with your ripe persimmons.

Don't threaten me with your volcano.
The sky is clearer when I'm not in heat,
& the poems
are colder.

In The Penile Colony

for Bob Phillips

Wearing my familiar worry wrapped
around me like a fur coat,
I walk out into the transatlantic air,
endangered species,
womankind in a world
of shivering men.

Kindness, worry, anxiousness-to-please
have been my nursemaids;
fear has suckled me
since I first learned to breathe.

But now the streets are strewn with beggarmen
who kneel
clutching tin cups & pencils,
strutting on their stumps
where legs once grew.

This is a curious world
changing so fast
that we are all babies
born in taxicabs.

That first great gust of air
which fills our lungs
turns blood from iron red
to inky black—
& never back.

A street of stumps?
A forest thick with cocks?
"Alice lost in the penile colony,"
you said.
But the forest is dying
(Uncle Vanya knew)
& see how those trees
bend & whimper
under their own dry rot.

Dying,
they want to kill us.
("Don't take it personally,"
the murderer said.)

We women will have to shed
our wraps of fear.
Kindness, worry, anxiousness-to-please
are luxuries our kind can no more wear
than fur coats.

In a rotting forest,
we are lumberjacks
raising our double axes . . . .

LYN LIFSHIN

it seems to me that a poem has to be sensual (not
necessarily sexual tho thats ok too) before its
anything else, so rhythm matters a lot to me or at
least before images even. i want whoever looks at
it, whoever eats the poem to feel the way old ebony
feels 4 o'clock in a cold english mansion or the smell
of lemons in a strange place, skin. . . i always steal
things i like from people   other poets   especially
from blues   old black and country blues   rhythms
lines so simple and true they knock you down.

Drifting The

things i have and
don't have
come from this
moving between
people like leaves like
smoke   i've been
waiting the way
milkweed i
brought inside 2
years ago stays
suspended   hair in the
wind   it seems to
float   even its
black seeds don't
pull it down
tho you don't under
stand how any
thing could stay
that way for
so long

Nine North Poems

Greenland, 850 A.D.

when the norse
came they didn't know
it was from a
different country
Lived together 3
hundred years then
stopped   neither
side thought
much of each
other   a few
hammers of
church bell metal
coopered tubs
with baleen

words   a few
eskimos learned
to write   medieval
runes   not much
else touched them
Then Europe left

they lacked true
warfare before
the europeans
no military
organ no special
fighting   regalia
murder occurred
sometimes over
a woman   men

beat their dogs
broke a sleigh
The most common
way of dealing
with antisocial
acts was to look
in the distance

numb with snow
many of the old
ask for death
from a son   a
daughter, the
corpse left on
the crust   the
men keep walking
toward greenland.
ghosts of the
abandoned burn
like foxes' eyes

the dead live in an
underworld that is not
very happy   like this
world but darker
they are hungry there
too   their one joy
seeing their soul
in the new baby's skin

the baby's soul
from a dead relative

nobody speaks
harshly or slaps

the child who rides
close to his mother's

nipple. Black
nights in bed with
his mother and father
touching each other

Someone always holds
the child   so

the dead won't
be offended   take

vengeance by causing
humps bowlegs or

large ears to grow

earth was a tent resting on
pegs with a cover over it
slashed by a knife in 4
different places to allow
the winds to escape   the
earth tilted after that   the
lost people live underneath

Sedna

long hair tangled
with sin   she is
hostile   animals
created from her
limbs make the
stumps hurt when
anybody sins.
Where the right
eye should be
there is hair
The sins of men
rain down like
shit on her
black hair.
Miscarriage and
abortion make
her furious
unless someone
confesses

shivering in wet
clothes   longing
to leave   no
salmon letting
themselves be
caught   a

huge sin must
have floated down
to the floor
of the sea

like dandruff in the
hair of the goddess

the shaman will have
to go suck on the
evil   spit it
out a pebble
stone

man in the moon
directing tides
eclipses earthquakes
falling snow

wild caribou live
in his house   he

has pigeon holes
for filing away the
souls of land animals
keeping track of orphans

men's sins go up to him
as smoke that burns his eyes

Wildflowers, Smoke

1
baby i want to see yr
thing is it   oh you're
so good to   do you
like my meat in yr mouth

2
sunday the green vines
catching the water. Leaning
against them   the
wet berries

i left before it got light.
All day you lie in the sun
near the falls washing the
night off (are all southern
men as suspicious of what
they can get)

later i wrote you from
rome knowing you have
no place in my life
except you're so symbolic

3
is that why the poems are
fragments   are pieces   i've
been wanting them to
connect the way
i've been wanting my
life to. But it's
all milkweed

4
even the first night
you said we can't.
Tuesday, flutes and
bells clarinets
rain on the slanted
roof   if i get up   do
anything too fast
in here   the way i
did with you (my hair
catching in yr lips)
everything starts spinning

5
yr small bones
choctaw indian
spider medallion
scraping our skin.
It's been hard for you
all night you
say does this
choke you

6
fingers like
yours always
let go. i need
a new black
cat bone. smoke
in the air   i've
been here before
blown by night

7
nothing in my
life grows out of
itself like
quartz

tho i've wanted to
write poems that
do   but they're

more like
wildflowers too
wind songs   rooting
in abandoned places

barry   is that why i
chose men like you
dark places   deserts
no settling down
safe gardens with
fences like rhyme

PAT LOWTHER

I see the women's revolution as part of a new outreach
of consciousness. The liberation of women from imposed
self-images *is* happening. Even the most hostile and fearful
women are absorbing it subliminally right along with the

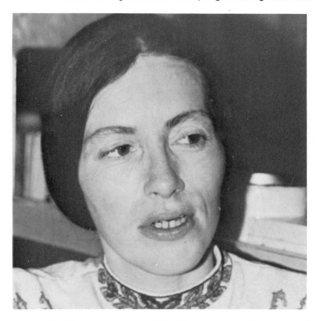

cream depilatory commercials. New assumptions are being
accepted below the level of consciousness. Then maybe
our poems, maybe some of the poems in this book,
provide the "shock of recognition."

At one time I believed we humans were coming to the end
of our evolutionary cycle—devolving like dandelions. Now I
see the half-breeds of the future passing like migrating
birds, and I begin to have a kind of tentative hope. Maybe
they'll find some clear space for consciousness, for going
on. Not that I wholly trust them to be right. It's too easy
to be wrong when you've grown in a culture that functions
basically by mind-manipulation. Maybe we have to go
through the whole trial-and-error thing again. After all,
that's how we got here in the first place.

Morality Play

Watching the light
people exchange
lovers easily pleasantly—
no fuss
no melodrama—
I think god
how sensible
probably fun too

I never lie
with any man but
we grow
tangled inside
each other
a jumbled knot that
fabulists could cut
their tongues on

Is it some
consolation that
I'm a woman
no one has
ever taken
lightly?

The Piercing

You will be beautiful now
as woman should be.
You will move your long neck
and jewels will sway.
As woman should be
a pure chemical
breaking the bland compound
of conversation,
you will turn your head
and sever light
into its elements.

Men will drink
pure red and indigo
from your throat.
Now you are truly woman
said the middle-aged jeweller,
plunging the needle through.

Remembering How

Remembering how
in the first luscious heat of sex
he was his own hothouse,
grew sensitivities
envied by all his friends,
his pen a green burdock
tickling the legs of passers-by,
implanting little barbs,
the seeds of private fantasies
(for every woman knows
a good man when she sees one,
he believed)

Now
that the juice is turned down somewhat
and mornings his root's a little numb
with frost
he still wears tongue on sleeve
his pen's half-cocked
up every skirt
no matter how
unpromising

He feels
if only he can keep it up,
his hand
on some sumptuous ultimate knee
will impregnate
a whole culture.

The Earth Sings Mi-Fa-Mi

(. . so we can gather even from this
that Misery and Famine reign on
our habitat. — Joannes Kepler,
a footnote to Harmonice Mundi.)

Outside the U.S. Consulate
in freezing wind
the street theatre group
arranges space within
the crowd

The girl who represents
the Vietnamese people
wears a black body
stocking and a mask
I thought at first
patronizing
but as the mime unfolds
its over-human contours
and its broken eyes
immovable
become a perfect image
for us all

Those of us near
the players sing with them
softly shouldering aside
our inhibitions
Ho Ho Ho Chi Minh
hoping our soft noise
will spread outward
from the centre

But the wind screams
and the earth spinning
like notes uttered
from whipped wires
the earth sings Mi-Fa-Mi

Regard To Neruda

When I heard that
the world's greatest poet
was running for president:
being north american
I would have laughed, until
I thought of the campaign trek
over country that was
his blood and bed,
and persistant human song
for which he became
rivers, harps of forests,
metallic skies of cities.
and I thought also
of the tenderness implied
in his handshake.

Could I see with his high vision
(man with thick hands and belly
full of good things)
the naked feet of beginnings,
the sons of rare minerals
transforming the earth,
could I wash my country
with songs that settle
like haloes on the constituents
I'd campaign
to be prime minister
without kisses.

Often now I forget
how to make love
but I think I am ready
to learn politics

GWENDOLYN MACEWEN

Writing poetry is so natural for me it's almost organic.
I prefer to call myself a writer rather than a poet, since
I am involved with writing as a total profession, not
only as an aesthetic pursuit. My prime concern has always
been with the raw material from which literature is
derived, not with literature as an end in itself.

Animal Poems

1.

Watch me
I am moving through the cages of the animals
I am moving through the peereek of their cells
Watch me because
I am watching them watching you
They are holding your immortal souls in trust
They have watched you since Eden
They are waiting for their time .

2.

When the day bends over backwards
to bring forth the light
I must know by whose permission I inhabit this place
in the holy congregation of animals
and mortal stones

Nothing lives here that does not flaunt
the handsome secret of its death
Nothing dies here that does not first
defile the earth

This tree is sexier than anyone remembers
and the world was made
for flutes and Jews
for jackals and for bells

The sun though
Look
Denies our citadels

3.

Not to worry.

The birds falling from these nests into the mouths of
gorgeous cats are always falling from these nests like
lost particles of speech or the pared fingernails of
the Almighty

Make sure you know with certainty what day it is, and
why, to answer for all the green and falling things of
Earth

Neither break the afternoon into unequal parts nor heed
the false and orange gods who insinuate life

For we are green and ever falling from high nests of
wind, the secret houses of the sky, into the jaws of
gorgeous cats and flowers

Not to worry but be handsome and heed these

MARGE PIERCY

I want to argue in defense equally of women who want
to work to create a female culture and those who want
to contribute to what has been a male culture and
change it to a broader, less oppressive culture. We have
to take for ourselves the freedom to deal with what have
been predominantly female concerns—subjects men define
as boring—at whatever length appears to us necessary and

vital and in whatever style we find natural or comely.
We have to take the space and time to deal with these
subjects as honestly as we can—in honesty to our percep-
tions. We have to insist on being judged and on judging
each other, for doing our own work, not for having failed to
replicate somebody else's. We have to fight just as hard
to deal with subjects that appear to us to be neutral of
gender, from our own perspectives. We have to thrust
constantly forward to clear space for each other. For us
to feel competitive with each other is illusion left over
from socialization in this society. We are not competing
any more than the first two aborigines who walked into
Australia were competing. We create each other. We
make the space that other women will occupy. We save
each other's sanity. I think probably all of the women
in this book are working to make part of the same quilt
to keep us from freezing to death in a world that grows
harsher and bleaker—where male is the norm and the
ideal human being is hard, violent and cold: a macho
rock. Every woman who makes of her living something
strong and good is sharing bread with us.

In The Men's Room(s)

When I was young I believed in intellectual conversation:
I thought the patterns we wove on stale smoke
floated off to the great heaven of ideas.
To be certified worthy of high masculine discourse
like a potato on a grater I would rub on contempt
suck snubs, wade proudly through the brown stuff on the floor.
They were talking of their integrity and existential ennui
while the women ran out for six packs and had abortions
in the kitchen and fed the children and were auctioned off.

Eventually of course I learned how their eyes perceived me:
when I bore to them cupped in my hands a new poem to nibble,
when I brought my maps laid down over Sartre or Marx,
they said, she is trying to attract our attention.
I was offering up my breasts and thighs and cunt
rather more loudly than women are supposed to advertise.
I walked on eggs, their tremulous equal:
they saw a fish peddler hawking in the street.

Now I get coarse when the abstract nouns start flashing.
I go out to the kitchen to chat about cabbages and habits.
I try hard to remember to watch what people do.
Yes, keep your eyes on the hands, let the voice go buzzing.
Economy is the bone, politics is the flesh,
watch who they beat and who they eat,
watch who they relieve themselves on, watch who they own.
The rest, the rest, the rest is decoration.

High Frequency

They say that trees scream
under the bulldozer's blade.
That when you give it water,
the potted coleus sings.
Vibrations quiver about leaves
our ears are too gross
to comprehend.

Yet I hear on this street
where sprinklers twirl
on exterior carpeting
a high rising whine.
That grass looks wellfed.
It must come from inside
where a woman on downs is making
a creative environment
for her child.

The spring earth cracks
above germinating seeds.
Hear that subliminal roar,
a wind through skirts,
the sound of hair crackling,
the slither of anger
just surfacing.

Pressed against glass and yellowing,
scrawny, arching up to the
insufficient light, plants
that do not belong in houses
sing of what they want:

like a woman who's been told
she can't carry a tune,
like a woman afraid people will laugh
if she raises her voice,
like a woman whose veins surface
compressing the scream,
like a woman whose mouth hardens
to hold locked in her own
harsh and beautiful song.

Agitprop

To come up behind you
and embrace you in the chair
where you sit working,
is a guerrilla tactic.
I rush in on the unguarded rear
inflict my affection
and withdraw at once
before the forces of defense can mobilize.
It is unlikely in this manner
that I will seduce you.
However, some force of insurrection
hiding in your rough clothes
might be inspired to rise in revolt.
Thus my attacks can be regarded
as propaganda moves--
promises to the presumably oppressed
of interim relief
and ultimate victory.

Seedlings In The Mail

Like mail order brides
they are lacking in glamor.
Drooping and frail and wispy,
they are orphaned waifs of some green catastrophe
from which only they have been blown to safety
swaddled in a few wraiths of spagnum moss.
Windbreaks, orchards, forests of the mind
they huddled in the dirt
smaller than our cats.
The catalog said they would grow
to stand ninety feet tall.
I could plant them in the bathroom.
I could grow them in window pots,
twelve trees to an egg carton.
I could dig four into the pockets of my jeans.
I could wear some in my hair
or my armpits.
Ah, for people like us, followed
by forwarding addresses and dossiers and limping causes
it takes a crazy despairing faith
full of teeth as a jack o'lantern
to plant pines and fir and beech
for somebody else's grandchildren,
if there are any.

What You Waited For

You called yourself a dishwater blonde,
body warm and flat as beer that's been standing.
You always had to stand until your feet were sore
behind the counter
with a smile like an outsized safety pin
holding your lips off your buck teeth.

Most nights alone or alone with men
who wiped themselves in you.
Pass the damp rag over the counter again.
Tourist cabins and roadhouses of the deaf loudmouth,
ponds where old boots swim and drive-in moons.
You came to see yourself as a salesman's bad joke.
What did you ever receive for free
except a fetus you had to pay to yank out.

Troubles cured you salty as a country ham,
smoky to the taste, thick skinned and tender inside
but nobody could take nourishment
for lacking respect.
No husband, no baby, no house, nobody to own you
public as a ashtray you served
waiting for the light that came at last
straight into the windshield on the highway

Two days later the truckers are pleased.
Your replacement is plain but ten years younger.
Women's lives are shaped like cheap coffins.
How long will she wait for change?

Three Weeks In The State Of Loneliness

Here I am sitting like a side of beef in the middle of Kansas.
We've never been here together.
Nobody knows who I'm meaning
when I say your name like a charm.
It doesn't work.

Lawrence is lush in the gusty spring
with forsythia and redbud and flowering crab
all gorged with flowers at once
while lilacs begin to dye the air sweet as grapejuice.
The leaves thrust open drooping as I watch.
From the limestone ridge of campus
I squint over the broad dusty bed of the farmlands.

What can give me a taste of you, touch of you?
The hazel glint of your eyes in a student's face.
A laugh in the hall makes me miss a beat.
In a man I am briefly holding
I touch that sad muscled exaggeration of caring
that makes you plod, a camel with nine humps of gloom
that you have not yet quite
perfected the world and yourself.
Not to share my thoughts sheers them off, unravelling.
I have no connections here: only gusty collisions,
rootless seedlings forced into bloom, that collapse.

The long distance bill keeps eating the food money.
I try to take an interest, I offer my finger to be chewed.
I lecture classes on why monogamy is wrong
while missing you sews a seam across my forehead.
I am the Visiting Poet: a red unicorn,
a wind-up plush dodo, a wax museum of the Movement.
People want to push the buttons and see me glow.

My loneliness lights up at night, a bucking neon cow
dropping purple moos on the sky of Kansas like blimps.
On the prevailing westerlies they should go sailing along
to be sighted looming across the Bay trailing long groans from Boston

maybe by Friday or just about the time I'll be packing
all the troubles I could or couldn't cause
into my suitcase and getting ready to send myself back
to the center of my center,
open as a road and warm as a tongue
my love,   my friend.

The Ritual

I have burst into
what I have been taught
to call love
regularly as wild grasses
seed themselves,
the idiot abundance
of generations
of fruitflies.

Attention, please:
I am about to perform
a dance with sword and torches
noisy and hazardous.
Masked with the head of a cow
I circle whooping and somersaulting
braying till I drop
a wooden pillar
whom I call, my dearly beloved
and the others—the bystanders—
a fencepost.
"And your love,
what does he answer?"
Why nothing at all.
Do you imagine that wood can speak?

Letter To Be Disguised As A Gas Bill

Your face scrapes my sleep tonight
sharp as a broken girder.
My hands are empty shoppingbags.
Never plastered on the walls of subway night
in garish snake-lettered posters of defeat.
I was always stomping on your toes eager to stick
clippings that should have interested you into the soup.
I told and retold stories weeping mascara on your shirt.
If I introduced a girl she would sink fangs in your shin
or hang in the closet for months.
I brought you my goathaired prickheavy men to bless
while they glowered on your chairs turning green as Swiss hats.
I asked your advice and worse, took it.
I was always hauling out the dollar watch of my pride.
Time after time you toted me home in a wheelbarrow drunk
with words sudsing, dress rumpled and randomly amorous
teasing you like an uncle made of poles to hold clotheslines up.
With my father you constantly wished I had been born
a boy or a rowboat or a nice wooden chest of drawers.
In the morning you delivered clanking chronicles of my faults.

Now you are respectable in Poughkeepsie.
Every couple of years I call you up
and your voice thickens with resentment and shame.
It is all done, it is quiet and still,
a piece of old cheese too hard to chew.

I list my own faults now ledger upon ledger
yet it's you I cannot forgive who have given me up.
Are you comfortable in Poughkeepsie with Vassar and IBM?
Do you stoke your memory on cold mornings?
My rector, I make no more apologies,
I say my dirt and chaos are more loving
than your cleanliness and I exile no one,
this smelly hunting dog you sent to the vet's
to be put away, baby, put to sleep with all her fleas.
You murdered me out of your life.
I do not forgive, I hate it, I am not resigned.
I will howl at every hydrant for thirty years.

Riptide

Ocean, mother of all living,
at the turning of the next tide, turn on us.
Reverse the rivers.
Loosen the silt in the stifled estuaries.
Up the grand canyon of the lordly stinking Hudson let it flow,
rolling up the Mississippi, thundering up the Columbia,
a tidal wave in the St. Lawrence, up the oily Cayuga,
all the poisoned fish, the cans, the plastic doilies,
iron ships of the black plague sunk in your belly,
innertubes and strontium 90 and rusting cars,
the chemical pissing of the miles of squatting factories.
Shoot it right back upstream,
into the tributaries, back through the dams, over the falls,
into the sewage systems and up the pipes
right out through the faucets of every sink.

CATHLEEN QUIRK

Writers never know what to say about themself &
vanity does the rest of the silence.

Poem

The crow flies between your phone and mine.
You want to know what you are
to me.   Babe, you are my ride in the country.

"Hold Back The Edges Of Your Gowns, Ladies,
We Are Going Through Hell."
— William Carlos Williams

I am seeing
other men now.

They ring the bell
differently than you.

We hold hands
across the dark,

spread out
and move in single file.

Oh yes,
there's miles of room

for sleeping on the run.

The Law Of Falling And Catching Up

Trap doors take a Sunday afternoon drive.
Your dog shouts over the phone: Dream
Cheat!   Dream Cheat!   The city adjusts its
night harness to the corners of your mouth
so you and your lover kiss soberly: mouths
open, mouths opening, per second per second.

Bird Calls

Put your arms on your back
and lean into one hip
almost to the fall-point.

Composition

Y'know
even a cantaloupe has a cunt
So why make all this fuss
about queens and nuns . . .
there's plenty of love waiting for you
right in your refrigerator.

Collaborations

"It was such a straight dream."

I never wake up well
with your hand over my face
teeth in the tea yinyangyinyang
you standing on the doorknob
& leaning out: as if we were
married. Rain and sun
strike the skylight
like silver rings like piano

lessons.
I never wake up well
in the saddle of my tricky horse
you with your hat on your head,
I will *not* go to pieces,
New York, bed.
Will return see-
king you.

PHYLLIS WEBB

I no longer make statements about my poetry. The
poems will just have to speak for themselves.

Antisong

bitterness rolls off
my tongue
ancestors roll off
my tongue
family living and present
wet my taste buds
spittle of little
pasts
viscous attachments and
venom
words
heave off my tongue
heraldic caskets
     dog   eyes
       return   Orphic
            vomit   profundo

"It's a poor memory that only works backwards,
the Queen remarked."

from The Kropotkin Poems

Solitary Confinement

It is a delusion.
The cell is not quiet.
A tree falls in the forest
with no one to hear.
The forest is falling.
It hears itself.
The rain ineluctable
speechless and necessary.
The cell is a green tower
maggoty   damp   a sickness
being offered.
It is just a cell like any
other cell   barred
hard   very principled
and guarded.
Let my tongue hang out
to remember the thirst for life.
Let my tongue hang out
to deliver itself
of the bitter curd.
And spit
give me water for spit
then give me
a face.

For Fyodor

I am a beetle in the cabbage soup they serve up for geniuses
in the House of the Dead.

I am a black beetle and loll seductively at the bottom of the
warm slop.

Someday, Fyodor, by mistake you'll swallow me down and I'll
become a part of your valuable gutworks.

In the next incarnation I hope to imitate that idiot and saint
Prince Myshkin, drop off my wings for his moronic glory.

Or, if I miss out on the Prince, Sonya or Dunya might do.

I'm not joking. I am not the result of bad sanitation in the
kitchen, as you think.

Up here in Omsk in Siberia beetles are not accidents but destinies.

I'm drowning fast but even in this condition I realize your bad
tempered haughtiness is part of your strategy.

You are about to turn this freezing hell into an ecstatic emblem.
A ferocious shrine.

Ah, what delicious revenge. But take care! A fit is coming!
Now, now,I'll leap into your foaming mouth and jump your tongue.
Now I stamp on this not quite famous tongue

shouting: Remember Fyodor, you may hate men but it's here in
Omsk you came to love mankind.

But you don't hear, do you: there you are writhing in epileptic
visions.

Hold your tongue! You can't speak yet. You are mine, Dostoevsky.

I aim to slip down your gullet and improve myself.
I can almost hear what you'll say:

> Crime and Punishment
> Suffering and Grace

and of the dying

> Pass by and forgive
> us our happiness

Ezra Pound

And among the divine paranoids old Ezra
paces his cage unattached to the mode of doubt
replete with salvation he is 60 years old
under the Pisan sunfire. He sees straight
through the bars into the court of Confucius
then slumps in a corner wondering what went
wrong. His old man's hair is matted with rain
and wardust. His brain is in fever.
Nevertheless he hikes from pole to pole
to plot once more the stars of his fixed
obsession. It seems so clear. If only
they'd listened. They shine light all night
on the perplexity of his predicament.
He stares back, can't sleep, understands
nothing. Jew-hater. Poet. Intellectual.
A curious animal, a-typical, it reads and
writes, shaking and sweating, being so shut in,
the canto arising,
      "And if the corn can be beaten
        Demeter has lain in my furrow"
the mode of doubt imprisoned for ever and ever
in the style of its own luxury.

Treblinka Gas Chamber

"Klostermayer ordered another count of the children.
Then their stars were snipped off and thrown into
the center of the courtyard. It looked like a field of
buttercups."
          A Field of Buttercups—by Joseph Hyams

fallingstars
          "a field of
                    buttercups"

               yellow stars
                         of David
                                   falling

the prisoners
               the children
                         falling

               in heaps
                    on one another
                              they go down

Thanatos
          showers
               his dirty breath
                         they must breathe
                                   him in

               they see stars
                         behind their
                                   eyes

David's
          "a field of
               buttercups"

               a metaphor
                    where all that's
                              left lies down

KATHLEEN WIEGNER

I have lived in the mid-land of America all my life,
learning to deal with a scarcity of everything but snow.

Finally I turned away from landscape altogether except
as it maps my consciousness. The emotions I write out
of are common: fear, loneliness, anger, sometimes even
love. Because I have a Ph.D. in literature I try to avoid
references to same in my poems. I write songs, stories,
always wanted to be a singer a la the 40's and keep
waiting for a revival. I keep trying to get songs into my
poems, blues, folk songs, jazz—the poetess as one man
band. I teeter on the edge of romanticism which I keep
disciplining with irony knowing my great potential for
the sentimental—as obsolete a mode as jazz singing these
days. I read a lot, listen to the music and poetry of my
friends, and dedicate these poems to my lover, my
daughter, Christine, and my dog. I believe in blessings
and beatitudes even when I am screaming.

Proteus

Well, here I am and
he, there, we have
this act. Oh I know
his tricks; we know
each other well enough.

Once when I had him
down he changed to
a child, crying in pain,
crying "mother, help me"
and I believed him
until he had his hand
at my throat. Or once
as I held him, he grew
young and white
as a boy, whispering
"please, do it now."
I could not refuse
and lost my advantage.

Sometimes before we go on
he counsels: "It is political
to lose, the crowd is on
my side, give them what
they want and we can be
in the big time."
And then he changes to money,
to love, thousands of hands
applauding our carefully
worked out act.

People gossip, saying
we sleep together, that
we really love each other,
that our fights are never real.
They do not understand
that he never sleeps,
but stands in the corner all night
watching my dreams.

Four Untitled Poems

Now in the window
the morning light moves,
pushes through the thin
ground of grey as
relentlessly
as a seed growing.

Since all things
can be broken
I would break you,

since all things give way
I would break you
against me,
throwing you
out whole, to take back
the pieces,

some things being better
broken; pomegranates
where succulence
glistens under the tough
skin, geodes splitting shine
with rare crystals.

In love you are
as sudden and as
surprising as
sometimes
the full weight of rain

I stand in
wanting no shelter.

Knowing I would say yes,
knowing that
let all the ocean in,
the sea-blood roaring,
my own blood at flood-tide
salty and warm.

For The Woman Who Asked Me If I Believe In God
And If I Pray

Kathleen Wiegner

Yes, lady, in the bright red suit
and careful grey hair, coming out
of nowhere one Sunday afternoon,
coming at me, I have taught my daughter
that God is everywhere
                              even when she laughs
                              saying, "in my toast,"
                              taking a big bite.
God, lady, like sex, is something you can't avoid
so you do what you can.
Sometimes she thinks God is in a big airplane
                              digging the clouds
                              and an occasional glimpse of the ground.
But prayer.
That we haven't talked about because yes, lady,
I pray, like Christ himself prayed, in the garden,
that last night, knowing what lay before,
knowing but still hoping there was a way out,
praying for a way out, in sweat and darkness
he prayed. Not the way they teach you:
                              God bless mommy, daddy,
                              Bobbie and Jane.
                              And please, God, let me
                              have a pony for my birthday.
No one teaches you the other, the one you say,
sweating in the dark, the only one you really need,
hopeless and still hoping, on your knees,
pinned there by what you know but still saying
                              "let it pass."
No, I will not teach my daughter how to pray.
She will learn it herself. When the time comes.

No Dice

Black sunshine
in a cool black glass

it shines

mother said a man won't
want you if he knows

you're loose, sugar,
not the tight wrapped kind.

Father said a man don't
buy the cow
when he can get milk
through the fence,

but anyhow

black sun light
it shines
in the window
on the floor

can't remember when
I last opened the door
to anyone.

One day last week I
painted the whole damn
room white. Opened
the window and the
black
sun
light
shined in

shut it down
tight
O I could love you
but
no dice.

At Times

You would take
everything
I had

and say
you'd earned it

with your
young body
and occasional
concern

as if it were hard.

At times
you stand
at the bedroom
window excited
by the girl's legs
flashing in the street

as if I had not
been with you
all night long.

One time
you got excited
just talking
about them,

God, you said,
those short skirts
and I was lying
beside you
with nothing
on.

Silver Dollar

A woman never knows what a good man she's got
never knows what a good man is
maybe like her father only
he drinks less
maybe like her first love only
more faithful,
maybe like her second love only
more loving
maybe like her last love only . . .
a woman never knows
a silver dollar rolls
           because it's round
           round
a woman never knows
never knows what a good man she's got
never knows that a good man is
never knows the silver dollar rolls
because it's round, because
        silver dollar goes
        from hand to hand
        because it's round
never knows
never knows
goes
from man to man.

FRAN WINANT

Being in the women's movement has made art, and
everything else in my life, meaningful to me. My writing
is part of a dialog with other women. I also write and
perform gay feminist songs. I started Violet Press as
part of the struggle to give gay women a chance to
communicate with each other and all women. My book
of poems is available for $1 from Violet Press, PO Box 398,
NYC 10009. We are publishing a lesbian poetry anthology,
$2, and an article on lesbians and health care, 50 cents.

Yesterday

(about Gertrude & Alice)

yesterday a lovely day
we traveled to the country
bouncing along in an automobile
the sun beat directly down
feeling it on my head helps me think
we bought melons at every town
until the car was filled
ate in a small restaurant
where the fish was excellent
fed the dog under the table
we returned at evening
to sit before a fire
smelling a fire-scent found in nostrils
not in air
pleasure swells from inside
to be made visible in things
that seem less than itself
in this way life is realized
through imagination

the present moment
cannot be described
without being changed
shadings of many days
make the moment that a poem is
that is why
the butter must be tasted
and the cow seen
again and again
it takes many books to equal
one taking in and letting out
of breath

a photograph caught us
walking our dog on a cobbled street

another caught us
standing in our garden
years later we are still there
new inventions
make the moment visible
but not in the same way as poetry

here
the curve of a melon
although eliptical
can be described as
an eternal circle
in which many rounds are represented
the curve of the sky, hills
and aspects of ourselves
can thus innocently be
handled and devoured
the sun that beats directly down
is like a certain light
that spreads from your fingertips
rearranging the world
as a painted canvas does
the smoothness of the tabletop
brings you close to me
although you are lying upstairs
asleep
the grain of the wood
is the line of your eyebrows

because you are always with me
it is not true
that I go off alone to write

Poem To My New Jacket

standing in the 14th st snack place
next to mays dept store
unable to escape my all-american reflexes
Im digging being surrounded by shitfood
watching the shopping crowd
black brown white female male kid adult mouths
all shovelling it down
some eating leathery bread envelopes
holding onions grease
bits of meat that are mostly cereal
and others eating pizza and knishes
this place has variety
Im leaning on one of those counters
where people eat standing up
with my big paper cup of black coffee
projecting myself onto
the outer edge of those taste buds
where the mozzarella cheese tomato paste
and crispy whiteflour dough
meet in a first steaming bite
Im on a diet after getting fat
trying to be a vegetarian
the way these people are getting fat on shit
carbohydrates did it
making me want to eat more
fatness is a form of starvation where
the more you eat the hungrier you get
and not for everyone but for me
it stands in the way of being able to believe
I can make my body strong
there was lots of nutrition
in the nuts rice honey and seeds
but they did me in
as surely as this gleaming shit
the ultimate come-down:
Im on a high protein diet meaning meat
and not eating in places like this
when I go back to vegetarianism
I promise myself I'll take a new approach
stop the shitfood joy-popping attitude
and plan meals the way its explained
in Diet For A Small Planet

which I read too late to save myself this time
meanwhile
Im watching with the kind of fascination
that turns life into art
involvement that holds small details
making them stand for everything
as in a dream
since last christmas
when the bathroom ceiling fell
Ive felt Ive been living past
one of the possible dates for my death
and in this place too I feel like a spirit
standing next to but outside life
having the same needs and physical sensations
as these people
knowing intimately what a mouth is
and the slow or quick massage of eating
but having no mouth
I think perhaps this experience will prepare me
for the spiritual side of vegetarianism
which Im beginning to see has to do with
putting a positive value on hunger
not starvation but a little unfilled hunger
all the time
its something vegetarians dont talk about

leaning on the snack bar counter
I kick the white cardboard box at my feet
to make sure its still there
inside is a snappy $8 ski type jacket
called a flight jacket and made mostly of
reprocessed and unknown fibers
according to the tag hanging from the zipper
standing here with bitter coffee
in early winter daylight
Im going to take 10 minutes to gloat over
being able to get my hands on
such a desirable dyke item
Im going to wear it with satisfaction
fighting off my fears of
looking tough and ugly

enjoying my toughness
building on it not denying it
and if necessary enjoying my ugliness
affirming that too
last year I got my first pair of boys shoes
on Orchard st
this year went on my first shopping trip
to mays boys dept
who says theres no such thing as progress
had a long conversation with myself there:
maybe I dont have to buy my clothes
in *this* dept
maybe theres something just like this
in the girls dept
up the escalator to check
nothing and the closest thing is $10 more
will I look like a little boy now
or a little girl
or will I finally look like myself
in my particular combination of
the clothes I want
wonder if theres a way to look feminine
in this jacket after all
stand in front of the mirror
hands in my pockets
something about these clothes
makes me want to go along with
the wide shoulders and solid shape
Ive admired the image of strength
all my life
and theres real strength not just pretense
in useful clothes
we can all be butch now and dont have to
shove that part of ourselves
which isnt only a part
off onto other women or save it up in ourselves
for special occasions
last night I dreamed mays was having a sale
on butch roles
my sisters rushed to get theirs
average sized women like me

walked out of the store wearing
huge amazon bodies

two months ago I decided to get my hair cut
and left the Wonder Woman Beauty Salon
sporting the hairdresser Carols fantasy
of a modified 50's D.A.
"You look good with your hair back" she said
just in time for the Bring Back the 50's Dance
where after all my protests against
glorifying our oppression
there was Marge done up as a dyke delivery boy
complete with dark glasses in a dark room
a well greased real D.A. haircut
straight leg jeans a white T-shirt
cigarette behind her ear
and I realized again that
our oppression is our culture
or at least it has been
for many gay women up to now
the role thing and the bar thing defining
the only territory where we could live out
the lies that passed for our lives
instead of the lies
that passed for someone elses
so I left the dancefloor went to the bathroom
made my haircut into a D.A. with water
rolled up my sleeves to show my muscles
hunched my shoulders
put my hands in my pockets
went out and did the lindy and the bunny hop
my sisters called to me "hi, Butch!"
and it hurt
I felt it as a condemnation
and wanted to protest no no
Im not that masculine woman
Im only play acting
the real scapegoat martyr obvious dyke
oppressor of weaker women
is somewhere else
this distrust of dykes wasnt only in my head

it was in the way my sisters looked at me now
the sarcastic tone of their voices
yes they meant it when they said
we should all make ourselves over
but they also meant it when they showed
they didnt know what the right kind of dyke
should look like or how she should be treated
she couldnt be
just a certain haircut clothes mannerisms
she had to be
real skills real fighting power
but if she was actually strong
would she have to go around looking tough
and if she looked like that
should she be automatically respected
or laughed at as a phoney
out to impress other women
the most tangible part of being strong is
looking strong and at that point
reality and wishful thinking get mixed

I cant dance or talk away
the negative things I associate with dykes
but at least I can live with
having my hair and clothes the way I want
my sisters encourage me
in spite of their doubts
if I can change my body
if I can become really strong
I think we'll know the difference

I walk out of the snack place
with my package swinging in one hand
and my coffee which is too hot to finish
carefully balanced in the other
I feel a happy triumph over the world
as I walk with my long stride
I feel almost comfortable
I wonder if anyone on the street
thinks I look strange

Christopher St. Liberation Day, June 28, 1970

with our banners and our smiles
we're being photographed
by tourists police and leering men
we fill their cameras
with 10,000 faces
bearing witness
to our own existence
in sunlight
from Washington Maryland
Massachusetts Pennsylvania
Connecticut Ohio
Iowa Minnesota
from Harlem and the suburbs
the universities
and the world
we are women who love women
we are men who love men
we are lesbians and homosexuals
we cannot apologize
for knowing
what others refuse to know
for affirming
what they deny
we might have been
the women and men
who watched us and waved
and made fists
and gave us victory signs
and stood there after we had passed
thinking of all they had to lose
and of how society punishes
its victims
who are all of us
in the end
but we are sisters and sisters
brothers and brothers
workers and lovers
we are together

we are marching
past the crumbling old world
that leans toward us
in anguish from the pavement
our banners are sails
pulling us through the streets
where we have always been
as ghosts
now we are shouting our own words
we are a community
we are society
we are everyone
we are inside you
remember
all you were taught to forget
we are part of the new world

photographers
grim behind precise machines
wait to record
our blood and sorrow
and revolutionaries beside them
remark
love is not political
when we stand against our pain
they say
we are not standing against anything
when we demand our total lives
they wonder
what we are demanding
cant you lie
cant you lie
they whisper they hiss
like fire in grass
cant you lie
and get on with the real work

our line winds
into Central Park
and doubles itself
in a snakedance
to the top of a hill
we cover the Sheep Meadow
shouting
lifting our arms
we are marching into ourselves
like a body
gathering its cells
creating itself
in sunlight
we turn to look back
on the thousands behind us
it seems we will converge
until we explode
sisters and sisters
brothers and brothers
together

PHOTO CREDITS

ACKNOWLEDGMENTS / COPYRIGHT NOTICES

LYN LIFSHIN — Three of "The North" Poems are from Poesias, one from Babyjohn Gets Shot On His Way To The West, one from Bugle American and one from Tractor.

PAT LOWTHER — "The Piercing" from Black Moss, "Remembering How" from THIS DIFFICULT FLOWRING (Very Stone House), "Regard to Neruda" from THE AGE OF THE BIRD (Blackfish, 1).

MARGE PIERCY — "In The Men's Room" from Aphra, "Agitprop" from Hanging Loose, "3 Weeks In A State Of Loneliness" from Hanging Loose, "What You Waited For" from Off Our Backs, "Seedlings In The Mail" from Hearse, "Riptide" from Good Times, "Letter To Be Disguised As A Gas Bill" from 4-TELLING (The Crossing Press), and "High Frequency" from Chelsea.

KATHLEEN WIEGNER — "No Dice" and "At Times" from THIS BOOK HAS NO TITLE   AN ANTHOLOGY OF MILWAUKEE POETRY (Third Coast Publishing), "Proteus" from Northeast and from Crazy Horse No. 7; other poems from ENCOUNTERS (Membrane Press).

FRAN WINANT — "Christopher Street Liberation Day" from LOOKING AT WOMEN (Violet Press).